The Survival Guide for Sports Moms

T-Ball to Tuition

by

Tracey Luebbers

Bloomington, IN Milton Keynes, UK

authorHOUSE™

AuthorHouse™
1663 Liberty Drive, Suite 200
Bloomington, IN 47403
www.authorhouse.com
Phone: 1-800-839-8640

AuthorHouse™ UK Ltd.
500 Avebury Boulevard
Central Milton Keynes, MK9 2BE
www.authorhouse.co.uk
Phone: 08001974150

First published by AuthorHouse 6/14/2006

ISBN: 1-4259-2425-5 (sc)

Library of Congress Control Number: 2006903853

Printed in the United States of America
Bloomington, Indiana

This book is printed on acid-free paper.

**This book is dedicated to my two sons
Dusty & Eric Luebbers**

**I Love You!
Mom**

I would like to thank my husband,
Marty Luebbers for his
contribution to the Positions & Terminology
chapter and the Coaches Corner. I also want
to thank my friend Dorothy McKeen for her
inspiration and friendship during the writing
of the book.

Table Of Contents

Introduction

If you're like me, you worry about your child's health and safety in sports. I feel like it is my job to keep them healthy and safe. Nutritional foods, drinks and proper rest are just part of doing this job. There are other obstacles to worry about. Is the equipment properly broke in? Is it fitted correctly? Is the coach handling the kids right? Is he/she taking into consideration the age group? Are the group of parents and their kids setting the right example for me and my child? All of these things and more can make or break the love of the game and change the way your child looks at life. Sports can teach children much more than how to kick or throw. If properly introduced, sports can teach your child life lessons. Team work, discipline, how to work toward a goal, good character, self control are just a few of the valuable lessons they can learn. Over the years we have used the lessons we have learned playing sports to help raise our boys. I am very proud of them. They have grown up to be responsible, hardworking, smart people. Playing sports had a lot to do with that, but not all of it. Having their parents involved in their lives played the biggest role in the men that they have become. Getting involved in what they enjoy doing, whatever it may be, is the greatest gift you can give to them. I hope you find that this book helps you to be ready for the challenge of being a "Sports Mom". The best job on earth!

PLAY BALL!

Tips For Moms

The Sports Mom's Survival Kit

You now live out of your car! I have learned over the years that having the following list of things in your car will make this "Sports Mom" lifestyle less stressful!

- This Book!
- Cooler with iced down drinks and water.
- Plastic sandwich bags to ice down aches and pains or injuries.
- Plastic wrap to keep sandwich bags in place.
- Towels
- A change of clothes for you and your child. Don't forget socks.
- Extra cleats or whatever extra equipment you might have.
- Folding chairs.
- Umbrella/Raincoat.
- First aid kit (with Benadryl, Ibuprofen and sore muscle rub)
- Roll of paper towels
- Sunscreen and lip balm
- Bug repellent
- Visors or caps
- Magazines to read.
- Notepad and pen.
- Healthy snacks
- Fabric freshener
- Team Roster
- Game Schedule
- Throw Blanket/Coats

Have their favorite CD's in the car.

My boys got pumped for the game by listening to their music on the way to the game!

Take along plastic bags when traveling.
These will come in handy for wet or dirty shoes, cleats or uniforms.

An Old Tissue Box makes a good dispenser.

More tips:

Hang your child's game schedule on the refrigerator at home and use a highlighter pen to highlight his/her games. This will help you make sure you are on the right line. Usually there are many teams on the same schedule. Also, be sure to write the games and times on your calendar at work.

Wash out and save milk jugs. Fill with water and freeze them, they make a great way to cool things in your cooler and you won't have to stop for ice before the game. Then during and after the game you will have very cold drinking water as it thaws out. If you don't have time to save jugs just freeze the sports drinks or water. They will thaw slowly and be ready after the game.

Stuff cleats with newspaper when not in use or after each game, especially if they are wet. This will keep them smelling better and dry.

A fabric softener sheet is a bug repellent. Place one in your pocket and don't worry about insect bites.

Cut oranges into four sections and place in large Ziploc bags, put in the sideline cooler for the team's half-time snack. Grapes are also good for half time. No trash on the sidelines to deal with!

If you already own a large water cooler without wheels just go to the luggage section in a store and pick up a luggage cart. Secure the cooler on the cart with bungee cords. This makes transporting the big heavy cooler much easier.

A fun way to reward your team after the game is to buy canteens. You can sometimes find these in the shape and color of the game ball. Write players' names on each canteen with a permanent marker. Fill each one at home with water or a flavored drink mix and keep in cooler until after the game. They will love running over and picking their canteen out!

To help me remember things such as drinks for the game. I put my car keys in whatever I need to remember, like inside of the refrigerator or in the sack with the snacks.

Do something for yourself, ask another mom to walk with you during the practice time. This is an easy way to carve out some fitness time for yourself.

Don't buy a new glove if you can find a used or handed down one, especially for the younger players. New gloves are stiff and take time to soften. The handed down glove will already be broken in.

If I could not be at the game when my boys were younger I would take something of mine (I used an angel pin) and put it at the top of the waistband of their shorts or pants. I would make sure it could not be seen but they knew it was there and so were my thoughts and love.

Write their name on everything! It does not seem to matter what age they are because they will still lose clothes and equipment. This will also help the younger ones find their hat, glove, ball etc., during the game.

Don't miss a great shot or the game! Offer to pay a family member or sibling of another team mate a few dollars to video or take pictures for you. They will like to make a few extra dollars and you won't miss a minute of the game.

If your child plays soccer, the shin guards can have a bad odor after much use. Use odor removal spray on them. It should take out the smell. You can use this on cleats also.

We learned this the first year going into high school. It's probably a good idea to make an appointment with your doctor for a physical right before school starts. This will save you the hassle of a long wait in the doctor's office, because every athlete has to have one before they can participate in a school sport.

When you go to purchase a chair to take with you to watch the game, I have found that the woven aluminum chairs are best. They are lighter to carry; cooler to sit in and you don't have to try to put them back in a bag!

Laundry Tips

For Mud, Clay, Blood And Grass Stains

Trying to keep the uniform looking good is difficult. Mud, clay and grass stains can make it look dull and dirty. Here are some solutions that I have found helpful over the years.

- Dishwasher detergent. Use the same amount you would use in your dishwasher. This will help get out mud and red clay. If the garment is white also use bleach with the dishwasher detergent.
- Regular dish soap, any brand.
- Rust remover, the kind that is in the laundry section of the store. This will help remove the red clay stains.
- Greased Lightning Cleaner.
- Biz detergent. Put the recommended amount of detergent and the uniform in cool water as soon as you get home. Let soak overnight and wash as usual the next day.
- Be sure to read care instructions on the label. Some uniforms are treated with special chemicals to reduce staining. They might recommend that you only wash in cold water without softener and bleach.

It is best to wash the uniform as soon as you can. Stains will come out better if they are treated and washed right away. I would always wash the uniforms right when we would get home and have it all together for the next game. This will help you just in case you have to replace something before the next game.

Equipment you many need to purchase

When you sign your child up to play sports there are a few pieces of equipment that the recreation department provides but be prepared to purchase a few things yourself. Each sport also has different shoes or cleats. <u>Not all cleats are the same,</u> be sure to be specific about which sport you are purchasing them for. The store employee should be able to help you make sure you are getting the right shoe for the right sport. Here is a list of items you may have to purchase:

Equipment for Football

- A mouth piece. Read the directions on the package because they usually need to be boiled to soften it then fit to your child's mouth.
- Football cleats. Remember to wear them some before the first practice to break them in.

Equipment for Baseball

- Baseball Glove. If you can find a used one that would be better than a new one if for a younger child. The best way to break in a glove is to just use it. Some gloves have directions with them telling you how to break in their glove.
- Baseball Cleats.
- Baseball Socks. These are different from soccer socks. They are not as long and sometimes a little thicker.
- Sliding Pants with a Cup. You can now buy the pants that have a place built in for the cup. Cups are usually purchased separately and come in various sizes. Take your child along with you on this purchase.
- Baseball Bat. This is an optional purchase because most recreation departments supply the team with them. As your player gets older he might want a particular kind. Get advice from someone that knows about

this subject. There are many different sizes, weights, and lengths. There are also rules for what size bat each age group can use. Be prepared to have sticker shock, some can be very expensive!

- Baseballs. Don't forget these! Have a few on hand, they have a way of disappearing. They always did around my house.

Equipment for Soccer

- Soccer Cleats. As before make sure you are getting the correct ones for soccer. Older players will want different cleats for different field conditions. They have cleats for soft ground and firm ground. Soccer cleats are a very personal preference. Each player on the team might have different ones on. This is very typical.
- This is very important! Do not allow your male child under any circumstances to wear boxers while playing soccer. Boys need to be supported because of all the running. Make sure they either wear briefs, boxer briefs, sliding pants or some sort of snug fitting undergarment.
- Shin Guards. These are usually supplied to the team. Shin guards protect the shin and the ankle area. These are also a personal preference item as they get older. Some players like to ankle straps at the bottom and some just want the shin protection.
- Soccer Socks. These are different from other socks. They are a lot longer than regular knee socks.
- Soccer Ball. Soccer balls come in different sizes for different age groups. Check with you coach or sporting goods store for the correct size ball.

Equipment for Basketball

- Basketball shoes. These are usually what they call "High-tops". These come up higher at the ankle than regular tennis shoes. This provides some ankle support. When you child reaches high school or maybe even in middle school there will be a particular color and kind of shoe that will be ordered by the school so everyone has the same shoes.
- Basketball. These come in different sizes too.
- Basketball hoop and Backboard Set. These can be purchased at any discount department store or sporting goods store. Some come with a pole and base that you fill with water or some come with just the backboard, net and pole. The kind with the water is the easiest to set up. This equipment is not a necessity you can take him to a public court or school and practice. But over the years the one in our driveway was really the best way for them to practice.

Other Equipment You May Want to Purchase

- Equipment Bags. For Baseball a bat bag is sometimes a good idea. This type of bag has a place for the bat and other equipment. Duffel bags or backpack type bags are very popular for other sports. Soccer usually uses some type of backpack equipment bag. My boys have always used and needed some sort of bag, especially if practice or a game is after school and they need to take it with them. It helps keep everything in one place and you can pack it ahead of time and know that everything they need is in one place.
- Insulated Water Bottle. Hydration is very important and they will need something to take with them to practice or games. Sometimes the team has a water cooler for the team bench, but it might not be enough to last the entire game. If it's hot, it goes fast! Send a water bottle for your child, that way you are guaranteed he will have enough to drink.

When traveling to games or tournaments with your child there is one rule you need to learn.

EXPECT THE UNEXPECTED!

Never leave home without the survival kit that is listed in the front of the book. Believe me those items will come in handy.

Schedules at tournaments don't mean a whole lot. Be prepared for them to run behind. Sometimes it is not the tournament directors or staffs fault. It could because of weather or some other uncontrollable factor.

In between games it is usually a good idea to take the team somewhere to unwind and that is cool or warm depending on the weather. It is best not to let them hang around at the field. They should get away and regroup. We have found this to be some of the best times when traveling with the team. This gives the parents time to talk with each other.

Always bring ALL of the uniforms if they have more than one. It is inevitable that one team member or more will forget their Jersey or socks of the color that they need to have for the game. Throw in any extra socks etc., that you may have. The coach will love you for it.

Bring more iced down drinks than you think you will need. This goes for ice too. If the game is running late this will save you from spending money at the concession and sometimes the concession will be out of drinks toward the end of the day or tournament.

If the weather is pleasant and you don't have much time in between games have a team picnic. Some tournament venues have picnic areas. Let each parent know what to bring or have each family bring what they would like. This will also cut down on sick or sluggish players because they ate too much or the wrong type of food shortly before the game.

The Team Mom

"The team mom" is something for which every mother should volunteer. Or maybe you will be asked by the coach; either way it is a much needed job. Most coaches are too busy with the kids to have the time to organize the team. Some of the tasks that are completed or organized by the team mom are:

- Making a team roster and or an information sheet containing player and parent information. This sheet could contain phone, address, cell phone numbers, etc.
- Filing any required papers at the recreational office or any state required or league forms.
- Collecting forms from parents or getting paperwork that is required to be signed by the parent.
- Handing out information that the parents need and keeping them informed about practice changes or any other needed information.
- Finding out uniform sizes of the players
- Picking up the uniforms and distributing them to the players. You could place each players uniform etc., in a plastic bag and put their name on it. Then just ask them to see you after practice and pick up their bag that has their name on it.
- Making travel arrangements for the team (if needed). If going to a tournament, sometimes they will have suggested hotels to stay in that would be close to the venue that you will be playing in.
- Collecting and keeping up with the money for the team
- Organizing the end of the year party
- Purchasing the gift for the coaches
- Scheduling volunteers for fundraising projects or concession stand
- Some teams require that you have forms on each team member such as medical release or birth certificate. I suggest that you get a binder and the clear sheet protectors. These items can be purchased at any office supply store. Place each player's information in each sheet protector and put in

the binder. This will be easy to keep and the information is displayed in an organized manner.

On the next few pages you will find examples of how to organize your team. Sounds overwhelming, doesn't it? Remember that some of the above can be delegated to other parents and take some of the load off of you. A well run team is a joint effort of the coach, parents and the team mom. Have fun with it!

Baseball Team Support Schedule

Date	Time	Concession	Gate	Drinks*
Saturday, March 1st	1:00			
Tuesday, March 11th	4:00			
Friday, March 14th	4:00			
Tuesday, March 18th	4:00			
Thursday, March 20th	4:00			
Friday, March 28th	4:00			
Saturday, March 29th	1:00			
Tuesday, April 1st	1:00			
Saturday, April 12th	12:00			
Tuesday, April 15th	4:00			
Friday, April 18th	4:00			
Tuesday, April 22nd	4:00			

Please come 30 minutes before game time if you are running the concessions. 45 minutes before game time if you are running the gate.

If you cannot fill your scheduled time please call another parent.

Thank you for supporting the baseball team!!!

* Please provide a cooler of drinks for the players and coaches.

Please bring 24 drinks and put your cooler in the dugout.

Name   **Home #**   **Cell#**   **E-mail**

Soccer
Information Sheet

Please fill in your information below, Thank you!

Your Name_____Home Phone #_____

Childs Name_____

Address_____Cell#'s_____

Work#'s_____

E-mail address_____

Please check or answer the following:

Is it ok to use your e-mail to let you know of any team information?_____

Would you like to help with the coaches end of season gift?_____

Would you like to help with the end of season party?_____

If needed can you help drive the team to out of town games and how many players can you transport buckled up?_____

What days of the week could you drive?_____

You could pass out something like this at the first practice. Take advantage of practices, they can be you best time to collect information or hand it out. Get your information at the start of the season and you won't feel like you are bugging the parents. Don't try to make a lot of contact at the games, the parents want to watch their child play not spend time talking to you about team business.

Tiger Uniform Sizes

Name	Jersey Size	Shorts or Pant Size	Preferred #
_____	_____	_____	_____
_____	_____	_____	_____
_____	_____	_____	_____
_____	_____	_____	_____
_____	_____	_____	_____
_____	_____	_____	_____
_____	_____	_____	_____
_____	_____	_____	_____
_____	_____	_____	_____
_____	_____	_____	_____
_____	_____	_____	_____
_____	_____	_____	_____
_____	_____	_____	_____
_____	_____	_____	_____

Player	Hoome	Player Cell	Father	Father Cell	Father Work	Mother	Mother Cell	Mother Work

Coaches — Home — Cell — Work

Team Manager

E-mail Address	Player															Coaches			Team Manager

Keeping Your Child Safe
And In Shape

<u>What To And Not To Eat Before The Game</u>

The last thing your coach wants to hear is "We picked up something at the fast food restaurant on the way to the game." The right foods are just as important to an athlete as his or her equipment. The proper food and times to serve it may be the factor of how your child will feel and perform.

<u>Good foods before the game</u>

Water or sport drinks
Fruit
Deli sandwich
Grilled chicken sandwich
Salad, (green, pasta or fruit)
Granola bars/Fruit & grain bars

<u>Bad foods before the game</u>

Carbonated Drinks
Fried Foods (french fries)
Hamburger
Fried chicken sandwich
Spicy foods (tacos, pizza)
Candy Bars or cookies

Other good rules to follow are to be careful what they eat directly after the game. Avoid real heavy, greasy, or spicy foods. It can make them feel bad or possibly sick at their stomach. Also avoid any milk based food or drinks. Especially if the weather is hot.

These are some suggestions to help your child feel better during and after the game. The right foods, eaten at the right time, will also keep them healthier and in better shape. These types of food decisions are good anytime and will teach them to **eat right for life**!

Be sure to have your athlete remove cleats and socks after the game before getting into the car. This will save your car interior from mud and clay. This is important, it will get their feet dry and prevent skin from pealing which can cause trouble throughout the season with blisters.

In the case of an injury or just sore muscles you should use ice. The best way to administer the ice is to simply use a baggie and plastic wrap. Put the ice in the baggie. Place ice on the injury or sore muscles for 20 minutes then off for 20 minutes. Repeat once more. That should do it! Remember to always ice your pitchers shoulder and elbow immediately after the game. Your child will probably tell you that it doesn't hurt. Do it anyway, it will save him pain later down the road.

Prevention is the key to having a happy and successful child athlete. As they grow they might have what is called growing pains. I have found that giving ibuprophen before the game really seems to cut down on aches and pains after.

Remember Epson Salt baths? They really work! It will pull out the soreness in muscles and it is relaxing after a hard game. Just add it to a warm bath.

An antihistamine is always a good thing to have on hand in case of an insect sting, or you could also use ordinary table salt on the sting site, it helps take the burning sensation out of the bite.

Be sure to check with your child's doctor before giving any medication.

Float a piece of fruit or a bottle of a sport drink in their water bottle. It will be cold and ready for half time or after the practice or game.

A garden pump sprayer is a great way to keep the whole team cool. When it's half time or when they are on the bench waiting to go into the game, they can use it to cool off. The kids love to be the one to spray their teammates.

Purchase a team canopy. They are not very expensive and can go over the bench to help keep the team cool or dry. Buy one for the parents on the sideline too!

Prevention and Information

- If your child's urine is dark in color, rather than clear or light yellow, he or she may be becoming dehydrated.
- One of the biggest risk factors for heat illness is a previous episode of dehydration or heat illness.
- Drinking fluids before the game is just as, if not more important than during and after the game.
- Carbonated drinks should be consumed in moderation for athletes.
- Make sure the coach gives adequate water breaks during games and practice.
- Always monitor your child's hydration on and off the field.

Bananas Prevent Cramps!

Important Information You Need To Know

<u>Heat Stroke</u>

This happened to my son and it was very scary. Please read this and be informed unlike I was.

What Are the Symptoms?

<u>Heat Exhaustion:</u>

- Fatigue
- Nausea
- Headaches
- Excessive thirst
- Muscle aches and cramps
- Weakness
- Confusion or anxiety
- Drenching sweats, often accompanied by cold, clammy skin
- Slowed or weakened heartbeat
- Dizziness
- Fainting
- Agitation

Heat Stroke:

- Nausea and vomiting
- Headache
- Dizziness or vertigo
- Fatigue
- Hot, flushed, dry skin
- Rapid heart rate (160 to 180 beats per minute)
- Decreased sweating
- Shortness of breath
- Decreased urination
- Blood in urine or stool
- Increased body temperature (104 to 106 degrees Fahrenheit)
- Confusion, delirium, or loss of consciousness
- Convulsions

Heat stroke can occur suddenly, without any symptoms of heat exhaustion. If your child is experiencing symptoms of heat exhaustion or heat stroke **GET MEDICAL ATTENTION IMMEDIATELY!**

This information taken from webmd.com

If your child develops heat illness you should:

- ✓ First thing to do is get them out of the sun and into a cool comfortable place.
- ✓ Give them cool fluids to drink, like a sport drink or water.
- ✓ Take off any excess layers of clothing or bulky equipment.
- ✓ Put cool wet cloths on overheated skin or around the neck area.

In cases of heat cramps, gentle stretches to the affected muscle should help relieve the pain.

This information taken from webmd.com

Fundraising Ideas

Fundraising For Your Team or School $

- Invite a local celebrity to speak at you school. Have light appetizers and sell tickets.
- Ask a local business to donate something of value and hold a raffle.
- Open a spirit store at your school. Sell t-shirts, hat, chairs, etc. with the school logo on it.
- Have bumper stickers or magnets made for cars with your team name etc., on it. You can find these companies on the internet.
- Take pictures at the game and sell them to the parents for a donation.
- Sell Bar-B-Q or hamburger plate tickets. Sometimes local businesses with donate the food you need. 100% profit!!
- Host a baseball tournament or any other sport tournament. This is a lot of work be sure you have support from all of the parents.
- Host a Golf Tournament. Get one of the dads to take this on. This idea can be very profitable!
- Bake sale or car wash. This can be easy to put together but the profit might not be what you need it to be.
- Community rummage sale. Get everyone on the team to go ask neighbors etc., for donations.
- Do a media guide for your team and sell ads. A media guide has player's pictures, information about your team and the season schedule in the guide.
- Have a talent show at your school and sell tickets and concessions.
- Do a mystery dinner theater play. You can find these for sale on the internet or maybe someone you know is good at writing. Sell tickets for the show and dinner. Have team mates help with the preparing and serving of the meal. Maybe you could get some of the teachers to star in the play. The kids would love to see that!

Quick and Portable Concession Stand

You will need:

Tables

Crock pots

Extension Cords

Price List

Coolers

Microwave

Cash Box with change

Paper goods

The table should be large enough to serve the food and collect money. The second table needs to hold the appliances and food. Hotdogs in a crock-pot do the trick. Make sure they are cooked thoroughly. You should be able to charge between $1.00-1.50 for them. After they are cooked put the hotdogs in the bun and wrap with foil. This will make it neater to serve and it will also steam the bun. Another concession favorite is nachos. Buy the canned cheese at your nearest wholesale place and pore into a crock-pot about one hour before stand opens. I used to start this at home and just take it with me. You should be able to get $1.50 for these. A good money maker is popcorn. Sell the microwave popcorn bags. This way you do not have any paper goods cost. A good price for these are $1.00 each bag. The drinks should be iced down about a half hour before you start selling. Check out the paper for good deals on canned drinks, sport drinks and bottled water or ask parents to bring and donate them, depending on expected crowed size. If you are planning on a large crowd contact your local bottling company, but they usually need three to four days advance notice and this would only be for orders of 20 or more cases. They will save your back, they deliver. It is very time consuming and messy to use 2-liter bottles. Get six to eight different kinds of candy. Candy bars usually go for .75-1.00. After you gather your supplies, get some change and type or write up your price list. Be sure to keep all of the receipts for the supplies. You will need to know the total cost of supplies to know what your total profit is. Last but the most important task, schedule your help! Concessions can be very profitable if you are organized and don't try to be a restaurant or convenience store. <u>Keep it simple!</u> Don't offer too many choices and don't keep a lot of stock on hand. These are all just suggestions that I hope will help you get started. Some areas or schools have a concession already established. But if not, this is a great way to make money for your team or school and this works at any location. Good Luck!

<u>Other Ideas for Concession Stands</u>

- Buy BBQ pork or beef by the pound with buns make sandwiches and sell.
- Some chain restaurants will sell you their sandwiches at a reduced price to you then you can sell for a profit.
- Order pizza and sell by the slice.
- Snow cones are a big money maker, just ice and syrup. If you don't have a machine you can rent them. On a hot day you could make up to $50.00 per hour!
- Grocery stores that have a seafood department will sometimes donate all the ice you will need. They will even donate chips or drinks. Just ask and you will be surprised how generous they can be.

- Buy jars of the big dill pickles and sell them. Kids love these! Some concessions even freeze the dill juice in very small cups and sell those!

- Bring a cooler on wheels and sell out of that. Get someone to walk around with it, and you will be surprised how much this will help move the drinks.

- Offer "package deals" with a price break. For example, if you buy a drink with the popcorn and candy bar save .25.

- If you have other items to sell such as t-shirts or pom-poms have them displayed close to the concession stand.

- Get someone to grill hotdogs or hamburgers for the concession stand. The smell of the food grilling will drive up your profits!

- Have parents bring baked goods or a crock-pot of stew. These will a 100% profit for your school or team.

Fundraising

One of the most profitable fundraisers I have ever done is selling space on a banner to be displayed in our school gym. The kids love to see their name on it, businesses liked the fact that it is displayed year round and since it was only one large banner it did not make the gym looked cluttered. I would send out the information through the school office in one of their regular mailings and e-mail. The banner was a huge success and the school renewed it each year making more than 8,000 dollars in two years at a cost of about $600 for the two banners. The next two pages show an example of the flyer used to order the space on the banner and a picture of how the banner looked. You could take this concept and make a banner that could be displayed at any outdoor field too. Each year you should make more that the year before because as soon as businesses and people see it, they will want to be on it. Good luck with yours and get ready to start a new tradition!

COOL IDEA !

The Central Academy Booster Club is sponsoring a banner drive to raise money to air condition the gym.

Show your support for the Tigers by purchasing one or more squares on our spirit banners which will be displayed in the gym. Each square is 12"x 12" and available to Academy families for $40.00 each. The squares are also being made available to local businesses for $70.00 each.

**Academy Families
Thanks for your Support**

The Brown's	The Cook's
The Jone's	The Smith's
The Lee's	The Bell's
The Wood's	The Davis's
The Nelson's	The Lewis's
The Martin's	The Scott's
The Simpson's	The Clark's
The Daniel's	The Grace's
The Miller's	The Wall's
The Hill's	The Pitt's

GO JOE!
#5

**SUZY SMITH
CLASS OF
2007**

We Support the Tigers

1	2	3	4	5	6	7	8	9	10
11	12	13	14	15	16	17	18	19	20
21	22	23	24	25	26	27	28	29	30
31	32	33	34	35	36	37	38	39	40
41	42	43	44	45	46	47	48	49	50
51	52	53	54	55	56	57	58	59	60
61	62	63	64	65	66	67	68	69	70
71	72	73	74	75	76	77	78	79	80
81	82	83	84	85	86	87	88	89	90
91	92	93	94	95	96	97	98	99	100

**Local Businesses
Thanks for your Support**

ABC Rental
ACME Construction
Quick Car Rental
AAA Business Forms

Personalize Your Support

Please Return This Form

Name_____

Number of Squares_____

Check Enclosed_____ Bill Me_____

Write your
personal
message here

Team Parties

To kick things off or to end the season, parties are an important time to get to know everyone or to say good-by. Here are some ideas and examples for all age groups of how I got the party started!

The kick off the season and pool party was one that I had given for my son's soccer team at his school. (I have included an example of the invitation on one of the following pages.) If you don't have a pool you could ask another parent if they will give it, use your neighborhood pool, or check with your local college to use their pool, (be prepared to pay for lifeguards). I used e-mail to let everyone know about it and to ask them to send money to practice for the meal. The day of the party I picked up box meals from a chicken restaurant and handed them out as they arrived. No clean up, no dishes and everyone was happy. It worked great!

Another party idea is to have some of the dad's bring their grills to the field and cook out right there. After practice or the final game is a good time that you know everyone will be there. Ask each family to bring something. It really works best if you assign what each of them is to bring and don't let them choose. You want to make sure you have what you need, not all buns and chips with no meat to grill. This has been a fun and great treat for the players and the parents!

Plan a team picnic. It is an easy way to get to know everyone and give out or collect team information. This is also a good time to sell tickets or items for fundraising. Just have everyone bring their own food, chairs or blankets and enjoy the day!

Going out for dinner or maybe after the game can be an easy way to have the team party. Just make sure you contact each player's parent to make sure they will be attending then call the restaurant to make reservations. Let each family be responsible for their meal.

A fun way to end a season or to start one is to go to a professional or college game. I would collect the money from each player first then order the tickets on-line or at the local ticket office. Some professional teams have special nights for each county in your state. We have had some really good times and the kids get to walk on the field.

Minor league teams (if your city has one or one is near to you) are a better way to get closer to the game and players. We have called the team contact number and have had picnic style dinners before the game. Players will stop by and sign autographs for the kids. This is a very easy and fun for everyone including the team mom. Be sure to collect the ticket money in advance, I have learned the hard way this works best.

One year we celebrated the season with a mom vs. kids' game. This of course depends on the age group. I did this when my son was 8 years old and we had a good time and lots of laughs. Afterwards we went to a family's pool and cooked out.

Have a treasure hunt in your yard or on someone's land. We saved coffee cans and filled them with candy then buried them shallow using play sand. We told a story of how the treasure became lost before the hunt began. The kids that attend many years ago still remember that party!

Sundae and milkshake party for the hot weather sports. Set up a sundae/milkshake bar. Have ice cream and toppings set up for easy assembly along with blenders for favorite flavored shakes. I recommend you do this one outside on a patio for easy clean up.

Kick Off The Season
Pool Party and Dinner!

When: Friday, August 6th from 6:00-
                    8:00pm.

Where: Any Address & Phone #
                    You must RSVP by August 4th!
                    We will be ordering the dinners on
                    that date.

What to Bring: Shorts, Towel and $5.00 for each
                    Dinner and Drink. (If you have not
                    already turned it in at practice)

Parents Please Come!!! We have a lot of
information to cover for the upcoming season.

Easy
Game Night
Dinners

Easy and quick game night dinners

Corn Chip Pie

Just heat up some chili, canned or homemade you could even use turkey chili for lower fat recipe. Open an individual serving size of corn chips. Pour chili into bag and top with shredded cheese. You don't even dirty any bowls or plates! This is a favorite with my kids!

Mini pizzas

Top english muffins with pizza sauce and cheese. Add your favorite toppings. Place under broiler until the cheese melts. This is a good way of sneaking in a veggie under the cheese. Maybe beans or corn.

Slam Dunk Sandwiches

You will need bakery rolls (round, like a basketball), a variety of meats, cheeses and condiments. First toast the rolls and melt your choice of cheese under the broiler. Take out and let each family member dress the sandwich with their choice of meats, etc.

Quick Beef Stroganoff

1 lb. Ground Beef or Turkey

1 Bag of wide egg noodles

1 Can of cream of mushroom soup

1 8oz. container of sour cream

Brown ground meat, drain. While browning meat boil noodles. Add soup and sour cream to meat mixture. Drain noodles and add meat mixture into noodles. Stir well. Enjoy!

You could cook meat day before and save even more time. This is a favorite with my boys and they don't even like sour cream (but they don't know it's in it!).

Poppy Seed Chicken

1 lb. Frozen Diced Chicken (or you could boil your own)
2 cans of Cream of Celery
2 cans of Cream of Chicken
2 tbls. of cooking sherry wine (optional)
3 to 4 tbls. of poppy seeds
1 tube of Ritz Crackers

Boil chicken until done, drain. Mix remaining ingredients except crackers in a large baking dish. Add Chicken to mixture. Top with crackers and bake at 350 for 30 minutes.

Easy Chicken Tetrazini

2 large cans of chopped white meat chicken
2 cans of cream of chicken soup
2 cans of cream of celery soup
¾ of a medium size box of Velveeta
1 large box of spaghetti noodles

In a large pot start boiling the noodles. In another large pot combine the soups, chicken and Velveeta stir often. When noodles are done add them to the soup mixture. Mix well and enjoy. My boys LOVE this!!!

Pigs In A Blanket

This is an all time favorite of kids!

All you need are hotdogs (or little sausages) and a can of biscuits. Preheat oven according to the directions on the biscuit container. Wrap each hotdog with one biscuit. You could cut the hotdog and the biscuit in half to make smaller ones. Bake at the temperature and time recommended on the biscuit container. Add chips or fruit and you are done!

Sloppy Joes

It doesn't get any easier than this! Just brown ground beef or ground turkey add mix and serve on a bun. Add chips or mac and cheese and you are ready for some relaxation time.

Going to Camp

Camps are a great way for your child to learn many lessons. Independence, techniques of the game, self reliance, organization and discipline. Exposure to is also one of the reasons you might be considering a camp if your child is high school age. In any case, camps are a fun and rewarding experience if you know what to expect and what to take along. The camp you are going to should provide a list of necessary items but I have always sent these extra things along and they really made the boys camp experience a lot nicer. I hope these tips will help you be better prepared for camp and make your child and you more comfortable.

- Save the zippered plastic bag that comforters come in. These make excellent towel, blanket and linen carriers for camp.
- Another good thing to send is a mattress cover. Most camps are held at a school or college and the campers stay in dorm rooms that have been used recently.
- You might want to buy a solid air freshener. Dorm rooms can be musty smelling.
- Be sure to put their name on everything! Even if they are going with close friends items get mixed up and the kids can end up with clothes, etc., that does not belong to them.
- Small container of laundry detergent just in case they run short of clean clothes.
- Plastic bags or laundry bag for dirty and or wet clothes.
- Money. Just enough for their turn buying the evening snack, pizza! Most of the time the local pizza delivery place will be ready for the camps to begin and are very happy to oblige.
- Sports drinks, bottled water and snacks. After registration we always went to a local grocery store and pick up some of their favorite drinks and snacks. This will cut down on too much junk food and you won't have to send extra money for these.

- Don't worry about an alarm clock. The coaches usually have their own way of waking up the campers. And some kids might have one on their cell phones if allowed by the camp.

- Expect to buy the camp ball or many other items at registration. They will usually give each camper a "free" t-shirt, but they will have other items smartly displayed.

- Swim trunks or suits, beach towel or extra towel for swimming, and a small container of rubbing alcohol to put in their ears after swimming. You could buy the brand name after swimming drops, but rubbing alcohol is the same and much cheaper.

- Sunscreen. I would be sure to have a dry run on how to apply. Ears and back of neck have been a problem for my campers in the past.

- Broken in cleats. Do not send new cleats or any other new footwear. Blisters are pretty much a sure thing if they are not broke in. If they need new ones, buy them at least 2 weeks in advance and let them wear them several times. Send an extra pair if they have one. Sometimes their favorite ones might get wet and not be dry by the next day.

- Band aids or new skin spray just in case you do not follow the previous rule.

- Over the counter medications such as anti acids or headache medicines. I would only do this if they are old enough to understand the proper dosage. Sometimes the heat or the cafeteria food can be hard on the head and stomach.

- Decks of cards, magazines or any inexpensive games. Be careful sending game systems or DVD players. They could be damaged or stolen.

Coach and Team Mom
Gift Ideas

Gift Ideas for Coaches

- Have the team sign a ball have it mounted and present it to the coach.

- Make a pillow out of the team jersey and have the team sign it.

- Gift certificate for a dinner out for the coach and his/her spouse.

- Gift certificate for an overnight stay in a bed and breakfast. My husband received this one year. We loved the place so much and went back several times. We never forgot the team that gave it to us.

- If the coach plays golf, purchase a round of golf at a nice course. You could include an umbrella with his/her name on it.

- Tickets to see his/her favorite team or sport. Maybe include a lunch or dinner certificate.

- A plaque from the local trophy shop. Include the team photo on it.

- Gift certificate to a local sporting goods store.

- Frame the team picture and have the kids sign the matting around the photo.

- Make a scrap book for the coach using hand written letters from each player telling him what they think about the season or let them just write what they want. It can really be funny what the younger ones might say. You could include photos too.

- Buy a warm up suit and have "Coach" and his name embroidered on it.

- Buy a plain sweatshirt and some fabric paint. Have each child place their hand in the paint and put their print on the shirt. Write their name next to it. Use team colors or all different colors.

These suggestions are, of course, for the whole team to pitch in. You probably should give a least one week notice that you will be collecting at the next game for the gift. Most coaches coach on a volunteer basis. Some might not even have a child playing, and just coach for the love of the game. Always remember them somehow at the end of the season, and don't forget the assistant coaches. They need to know that what they do is appreciated and has made a positive impact in your child's life.

Team Mom Gift Ideas

- This book with a tote bag for her survival kit.
- Check out the beautiful creations on mommybraclets.com she will have it for many years.
- Gift certificate for a manicure and pedicure.
- Gift certificate for a massage. This is always a favorite! It's something she would never do herself.
- Gift certificate for a dinner out for her and her spouse. Don't forget about the spouse, I'm sure they have helped her or it might be the coach.
- Gift certificate from her favorite store.
- Moms on the team have a party or dinner out just for the moms in her honor.
- Gift certificate for a car wash/detailing. I'm sure she will appreciate this after a season of driving kids to games.
- Have a mom's get-a-way weekend and pay her way.
- Fleece Throw with team name and hers embroidered on it or a tote bag.
- A nice chair with umbrella. Buy one with the team colors and maybe you could even have her name put on them.
- A nice box of thank you cards. She should need these to send to all of the parents on the team because they helped her out so much!

Preserving Memories

Preserving Memories

- The easiest ways to keep newspaper clippings, ticket stubs, etc. is to put them in the clear sheet protectors in a binder.

- On the back of team photos or snapshots be sure to put the players' names. Years from now you might not remember all of their names.

- Another way to help remember all of the team members' names is to have them sign their name and number on a piece of photo frame matting. Then place the picture and the mat in the frame. This also makes a great coaches gift!

- A Mylar balloon placed on a poster board with the team picture in the center and framed looks great! Choose a soccer ball Mylar balloon or whatever sport your team is involved in glue it to the poster board have the team sign it and frame it.

- Tie cleats together, hang from hooks or pegs near team pictures or in your sports themed room. Be sure to write on or in the shoe the year and team name.

- Keep all of their team t-shirts or jerseys. They could be made into a keepsake quilt or they make cute pillows to decorate their bed or play area.

- If your child is lucky enough to hit a homerun, don't forget to fetch the ball. Most teams will let you keep the ball. Take a permanent marker and put the date and team you were playing or any other information you would like to be sure to remember. You could start displaying them using a plastic cover from the trophy shop or just by lining them on a shelf. Hope you have many to display!

- Save their gloves, batting gloves, shin guards, goalie gloves or any other small equipment items. These are good size items to display in shadow boxes in their room or your sports themed family room. You can make your own shadow box or go to the home improvement store or hobby shop. They have ready made ones.

- During your child's season be sure to check the paper daily. Your local paper should cover opening day, high school varsity games and sometimes traveling or club teams.

- An inexpensive way to display newspaper clippings, snapshots and certificates is to purchase the clear plastic frames and colored paper. Cut the paper to fit the frame (you could use team colors or scrapbook paper with the sport theme on it) center the article or photo on the paper and slide into the frame.

- Display jerseys on the wall with a wooden rod with brackets. Just thread the rod through the sleeves and neck and place in brackets.

Parents' Etiquette

Parents Etiquette

- Always support your coach. This will teach your child to do the same. If you have a problem with the coach, discuss it in private and not around your child. A coach can be a very important person to your child and this will help them to learn respect.

- Remember how you act and what you say affects your child in more ways than you know. Unfortunately it can also affect playing time and the way the coach thinks and acts toward your child. Be respectful all times on and off the field. The game may seem very important at the time, but I can guarantee it will not seem so important to you later. Don't embarrass yourself!

- A short yell of encouragement is always best. Don't try to coach your child from the sidelines. Try to always direct cheers to the team and not any individual player. For example "Go Team you can do it!" If you cannot do this, watch the game in your car!

- Learn the rules of the game. This will keep you from making any embarrassing comments. It also makes the game more enjoyable.

- Refrain from making negative comments or gestures to the officials.

- Be sure to volunteer to help the coach or team. Everyone's involvement is needed.

Ways For A Parent To Cheer For The Team

1. Looking great! Keep it up!
2. Way to go!
3. Good work!
4. Great idea!
5. Look at you go!
6. Good for you!
7. Keep on trying!
8. You did it!
9. Good team work!
10. You can do it!
11. You're doing fine!
12. Good going!
13. Great Job!
14. Look at you go!
15. I'm very proud of you!
16. I like that!
17. Excellent!
18. That's the way to do it!
19. Now you have the hang of it!
20. Beautiful job!

Sports Positions
And
Terminology

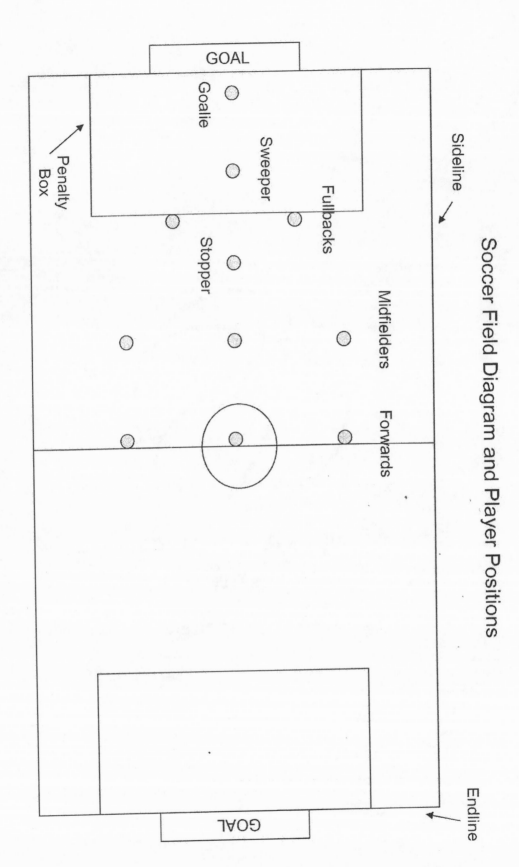

Soccer Field Diagram and Player Positions

Defensive Positioning

Soccer Field Diagram and Player Positions

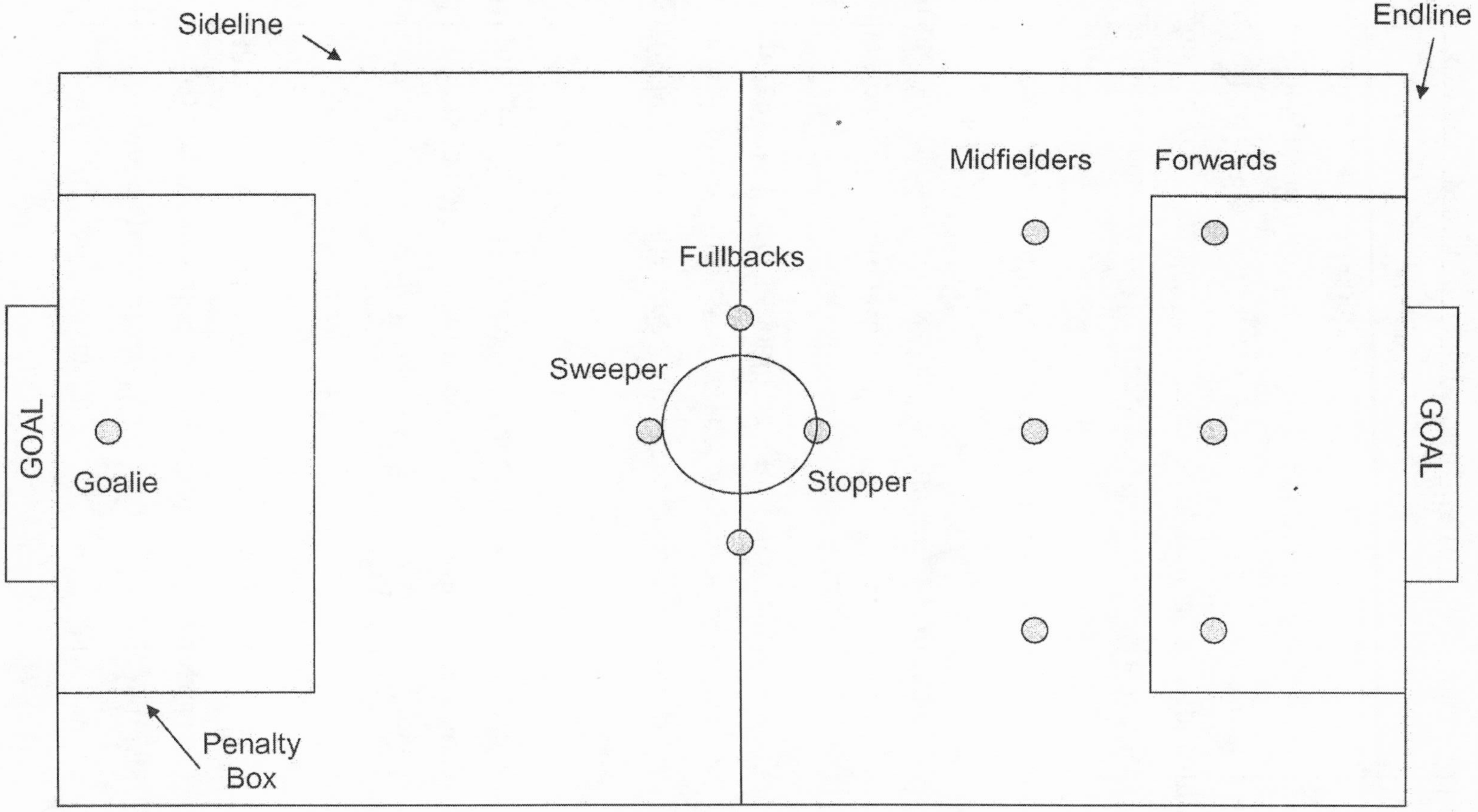

GOAL

Goalie

Penalty Box

Sideline

Sweeper

Fullbacks

Stopper

Midfielders

Forwards

Endline

GOAL

Offensive Positioning

Soccer Positions

Goalie: the goalie is the only player on the field who can use his hands and he can do this only in the penalty area. His job is to keep the ball from going into the goal. He also directs the defensive player on positioning. The goalie doesn't have to be fast but should have quick reflexes, good hands and good lateral movement.

Sweeper: the sweeper is the last defense between the opposing team and the goalie. He directs the other defenders and pushes them up field when the ball crosses the midfield line. The sweeper needs to be tough, fast and have a good vision of the entire field.

Full backs: fullbacks should mark or cover the opposing teams offensive players. Their job is to deny the offensive players a clear shot and steal the ball and advance it up field. Full backs should be strong and tough.

Stopper: the stopper is the first line of defense. He attacks the ball and tries to keep it on the other teams end of the field, passing to midfielders or forwards. He must also get back on defense and help defend the goal when the opposition tries to score. Stoppers should be aggressive, have a strong leg and be tough.

Midfielders: midfielders are the link between the defensive and offensive players. The cover both ends of the field and play defense when the opposing team has the ball and offense when the other team has the ball. Midfielders are usually smaller and quicker and must have a lot of endurance as they run the length of the field as well as good ball control.

Forwards: forwards primary responsibility is to score goals. They are the offensive players and should position themselves to receive the ball from defenders and midfielders so that they can take shots on the goal.

Soccer Terminology

1. Attacking team: the team that has possession of the ball and is trying top score.

2. Defending team: the team without the ball that is trying to stop the other team from scoring.

3. Goal: occurs when the ball gets past the goalie and crosses over the end line into the goal area. The scoring team is awarded 1 point.

4. Dribbling: the skill of advancing the ball with your feet while maintaining control and possession of the ball.

5. Clear: the act of kicking the ball away from one's goal.

6. Match: a soccer game

7. Corner Kick: a play in which the attacking team restarts play when the ball has been kicked out of bounds by the defensive team across the endline. The ball is placed on the corner of the field and play is resumed when the ball is kicked back onto the field.

8. Goal Kick: a play in which the defending team restarts play after the attacking team has kicked the ball out of bounds across the end line.

9. Marking: guarding an opposing player to either deny him the ball or preventing him from advancing the ball towards the goal.

10. Offsides: occurs when an offensive player positions himself to receive a pass between the last defender and the goalie.

11. Passing: ball movement between players of the same team that results in maintaining possession of the ball.

12. Penalty Kick: a play resulting from a defensive infraction inside the penalty box. The ball is placed directly in front of the goal and the offensive player has a scoring opportunity with only the goalie defending.

13. Red Card: a card the referee uses to signal a players removal from the game resulting from multiple rules infractions or violent or dangerous play.

14. Save: the act of preventing a goal by blocking or stopping a shot that would have otherwise gone in.

15. Slide tackle: a defensive play in which the ball is taken from a player by a sliding kick in which the ball is played through the possessing player.

16. Throw-in: a play used to re-enter the ball into play when it has gone out of bounds on the sidelines. A player must throw the ball over his head with both hands and keep both feet on the ground.

17. Yellow card: a card the referee uses to signal a warning to a player for unsportsmanlike or dangerous play. Two yellow card infractions in one game results in a red card and the players removal from the game.

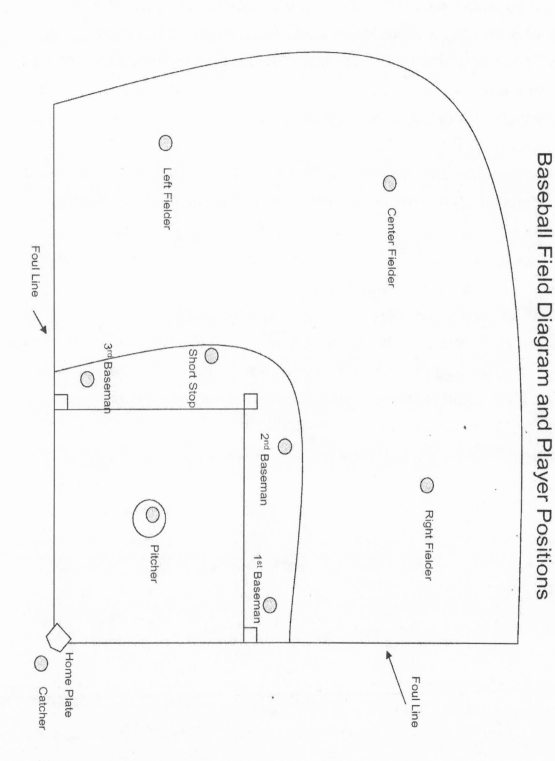

Baseball Field Diagram and Player Positions

Left Fielder

Center Fielder

Foul Line

3rd Baseman

Short Stop

2nd Baseman

Right Fielder

Pitcher

1st Baseman

Home Plate

Catcher

Foul Line

Baseball Positions

<u>Pitcher</u>: the player that throws the ball to the batter. The pitcher controls the tempo of the game by deciding how much time to take between pitches. This may depend on the pitchers personality or the game situation. Successful pitchers don't have to be the hardest throwers but must have good control, changing the speed and location of the pitches. When in doubt, staying low and away on the batters give them the best chance of getting batters out.

<u>Catcher</u>: catchers receive the ball from the pitcher. Catching is the most physically demanding position on the field as he must use his body to block pitches and keep them from going by him. They also should have strong arms to be able to make throws from home to all the bases.

<u>1st Base</u>: the 1st baseman plays close to the bag at 1st and is involved in most infield plays. He must filed any balls hit to him as well as catch throws and touch the base on other infield plays. Tall left handed players with good gloves are a natural for this position. This position doesn't require a lot of quickness, speed or are strength.

<u>2nd Baseman</u>: the 2nd baseman plays to the right of 2nd base and has responsibility for covering the bag on throws from the catcher, shortstop and 3rd baseball as well as balls hit to left field. He also must go into the outfield as the "cut-off" man on balls hit to right and center field. These players are typically smaller and faster than other plays with good hands. Arm strength is not as important as they have a short throw to 1st.

<u>Short Stop</u>: the short stop plays to the left of 2nd base and has responsibility for throws to 2nd base from the catcher, 2nd and 1st baseman and from the right and centerfielder. He also is the cut-off man on throws from left field. The short

stop is typically on of the most athletic players because he must have the speed to cover a large area, the arm strength to make long throws and very good hands.

3rd Baseman: the 3rd baseman plays just inside the bag. He plays the "hot-corner" because many balls hit to him are hit hard and fast. He doesn't have to have a lot of speed but should have quick reactions and a strong arm to make the throw to 1st.

Outfielders: the outfielders cover right, center and left field. They all have similar responsibilities that include backing up the infielders on throws made, covering a lot of area on either fly balls or ground balls hit in their area and have good arm strength to be able to quickly get the ball back into the infield.

Baseball Terminology

1. **Ball:** a pitch that the batter does not swing at and that is outside the strike zone.

2. **Double:** a play in which the ball is hit safely and the batter advances to 2nd base.

3. **Double play:** when two baserunners are put out on the same play.

4. **Error:** occurs when a fielder doesn't field the ball properly or makes a bad throw and a baserunner advances safely.

5. **Fair ball:** a ball hit in the field of play

6. **Force out:** occurs on a hit groundball when a baserunner must run to leave an open base for the batter. The fielder does not have to tag the runner, he just ahs to touch the base with his ball in his glove. A force out is always in effect with batter going to 1st base.

7. **Foul ball:** a ball hit out of the field of play. If caught in the air, the batter is out.

8. **Groundball:** a ball hit on the ground. In order to get the batter out, the fielder must throw the ball to the base before the batter gets there to get him out.

9. **Hit:** a ball that is hit in which the runner reaches a base safely and no error was made by the fielding team.

10. **Homerun:** a ball that is either hit over the outfield fence in the air or the runner reaches home plate safely without the fielding team making an error.

11. **Inning:** the length of play when each team gets a turn at bat.

12. **Line Drive:** a hard hit ball that stays in the air but does not get very high off the ground.

13. **Out:** when a batter fails to reach base safely or another runner doesn't advance safely on a hit ball. A team gets 3 outs per inning.

14. **Pop fly:** a ball hit high into the air.

15. **Run:** occurs when a baserunner safely crosses homeplate. A team is awarded 1 point per run.

16. **Safe:** occurs when a baserunner reaches a base without getting put out by the fielding team.

17. **Single:** a play in which the ball is hit safely and the batter advances to 1st base.

18. **Slide:** when a baserunner leaves his feet and slides either feet first or head first into a base in an effort to be safe.

19. **Steal:** occurs when a base runner advances to the next base without the batter putting the ball in play.

20. **Strike:** a pitch the batter doesn't swing at that the umpire calls within the strike zone, a pitch that the batter swings and misses or a ball that is hit in foul territory. A batter gets 3 strikes before he is called out and cannot be called out on a foul ball on the 3rd strike unless the catcher catches the ball.

21. **Strike out:** results when a batter either let's a pitch called a strike pass by without swinging or swinging and missing the pitch with 2 strikes.

22. **Strike zone:** the area over homeplate typically from the batters knees to just above the batters waist that an umpire uses to determine if a pitch is a strike or ball.

23. **Tag:** the act of touching a baserunner by a fielder with his glove with the ball in it while a baserunner is not on base that results in an out.

24. **Walk:** occurs when a batter gets 4 balls before he gets 3 strikes. He is safely awarded 1st base. This also occurs when a batter is hit by a pitched ball.

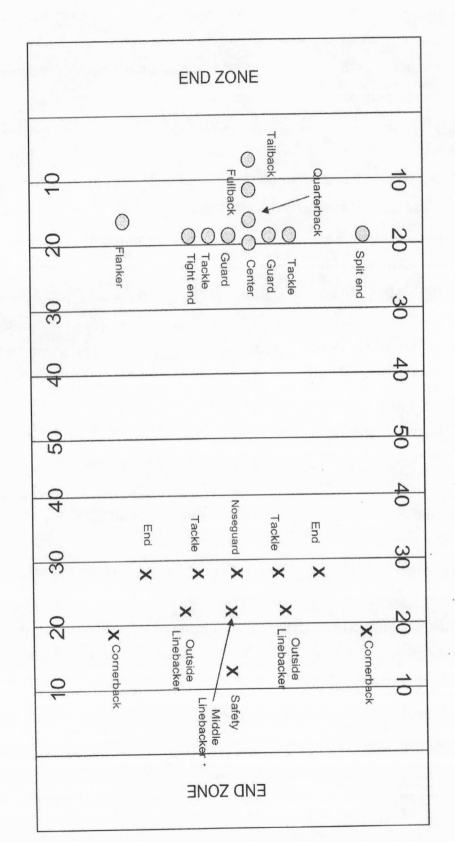

Football Field Diagram and Player Positions

Offensive Positions

Defensive Positions

72

END ZONE

END ZONE

Football Field Diagram and Player Positions

Typical Scrimmage Line-up

Football Positions

Offensive Line: I'll start with these guys because they do all the work but don't get any of the glory. They are the backbone of the offense and below I will describe the positions and their primary purpose:

1. Center – the center initiates every play by hiking the ball (placing the ball from his hands to the quarterbacks hands) to start every play from scrimmage. He not only has to make this exchange but also has to pick up his blocking assignment, either the noseguard or a linebacker. The timing and intelligence of this player is very important and he is a key player in starting every play.
2. Guards – these guys must be tough but also have some agility. They are the primary protection for the quarterback but also are required to move quickly and be able to make blocks on the run.
3. Tackles – the tackles typically are some of the larger players and have their primary mission to keep any defenders from tackling their running backs or getting to the quarterback.
4. Tight end – primarily used as a blocker but is the only lineman who is eligible to catch passes. This player doesn't have to have a lot of speed but should have good hands and agility.

Receivers: the split end and the flanker are the primary pass catchers on the team. The split end lines up on the line of scrimmage while the flanker usually lines up a yard or two behind the line of scrimmage. These players are usually smaller and quicker than most and have good hands. They must also block on running plays.

Backs: these guys get all the glory. They handle the ball on most every play but also have other responsibilities.

1. Fullback – the fullback is usually the largest of the running backs and is used primarily as a blocker for the halfback. He is usually used on short yardage plays to get the tough yardage.

2. Halfback – usually fast and tough, the tailback is the main ball carrier. Good backs have the ability to change directions quickly, have good vision of the field and are tough to bring down once contact is made.

3. Quarterback – the field general as he is sometimes called must know what each players responsibility is on every play. On running plays he hands the ball to the running backs or keeps it himself. On passing plays, he must know where each receiver is and make accurate passes, sometimes while being under pressure.

Defensive Lineman: "down in the trenches", these players take on the offensive lineman and try to either get to the quarterback or tackle the running backs.

1. Noseguard: his main responsibility is to try to disrupt each play from the beginning by hitting the center and plugging up the middle of the field. On pass plays, he has the shortest distance to the quarterback and tries to apply pressure quickly. Players that are big, strong and quick make the best noseguards.

2. Defensive Tackles: a tackles job is just that, to find the ball carrier and bring him to the ground. The also need to engage the offensive lineman to keep them from blocking the linebackers. Tackles need to be large immovable objects.

3. Defensive Ends: the ends have containment responsibility; that is the need to make sure they keep ballcarrier in the middle of the field where the rest of the defenders are. They are typically tall and have good quickness.

4. Linebackers: Usually the most aggressive players, linebackers have to have the speed of a halfback and the size of a fullback. The middle linebacker is the "quarterback" of the defense. Linebackers cover the field

from sideline to sideline and are also often called upon to cover receivers in pass coverage.

5. <u>Cornerbacks</u>: the cornerbacks primary responsibilities are to cover the receivers in pass coverage and to contain run plays inside of them. They are usually smaller and quicker than other defenders.

6. <u>Safety</u>: The safety is the deepest defender on the field and should never allow an offensive play get behind him. He must cover on pass plays and is counted on to tackle the ball carrier if he makes it past the other defenders. Must be fast but also have some size to him to be able to tackle tight ends and running backs.

Football Terminology

1. **Touchdown:** 6 points awarded to a team when a player carriers to ball into the end zone or catches a pass in the endzone.

2. **Extra Point:** after scoring a touchdown, a team gets the opportunity to receive one additional point by kicking a filled goal or 2 points by scoring form the 3 yard line.

3. **Field Goal:** 3 point awarded to a team for kicking the ball through the goal posts.

4. **Line of scrimmage:** an imaginary line across the field where the ball is placed. No team is allowed to cross this line prior to the start of a play.

5. **Down:** A team has 4 downs or plays to gain 10 yards. Failure to do so, results in the other team taking possession of the ball.

6. **Fumble:** a ball that is dropped or stripped from a player before he hits the ground, usually determined by when his knee touches the ground If recovered by the other team, they get possession of the ball.

7. **Pass Play:** a play in which the quarterback or other player behind the line of scrimmage throws the ball down the field to another player.

8. **Running Play:** a play in which the quarterback or other players try to advance the ball by running through and around defenders.

9. **Punt:** a play which usually occurs on 4th down in which the offensive team kicks the ball down the field to move the other team farther back from their endzone.

10. **Penalties:** infractions of the rules which results in the offending team giving up yardage to the other team. Common penalties are listed below:

   A. <u>Offsides</u>: a 5 yard penalty assessed when a player crosses the line of scrimmage before the ball is hiked.

   B. <u>Holding</u>: a 10 yard penalty assessed when a player grabs another player with his hands and/or arms. This penalty does not apply when trying to tackle the ballcarrier.

C. Clipping: a 15 yard penalty assessed when a player blocks a player from behind.

D. Pass Interference: a penalty assessed that maybe 15 yards or award possession at the place of infraction resulting from one player making contact with another on a pass play before the ball arrives.

E. Delay of Game: a 5 yard penalty assessed when a time takes more than the allowed time in between plays.

F. Unsportsmanlike Conduct: a 15 yard penalty assessed when a player conducts himself in a violent or inappropriate manner.

Basketball Court Diagram and Player Positions

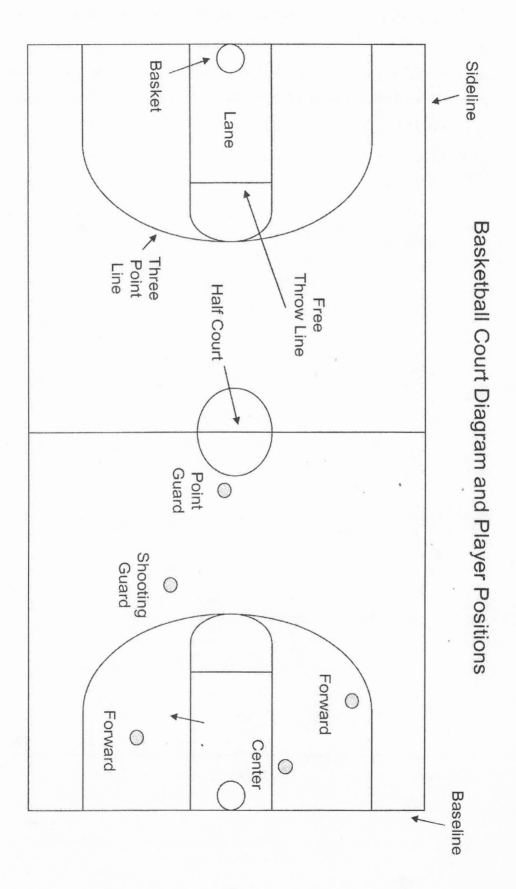

Offensive Positioning

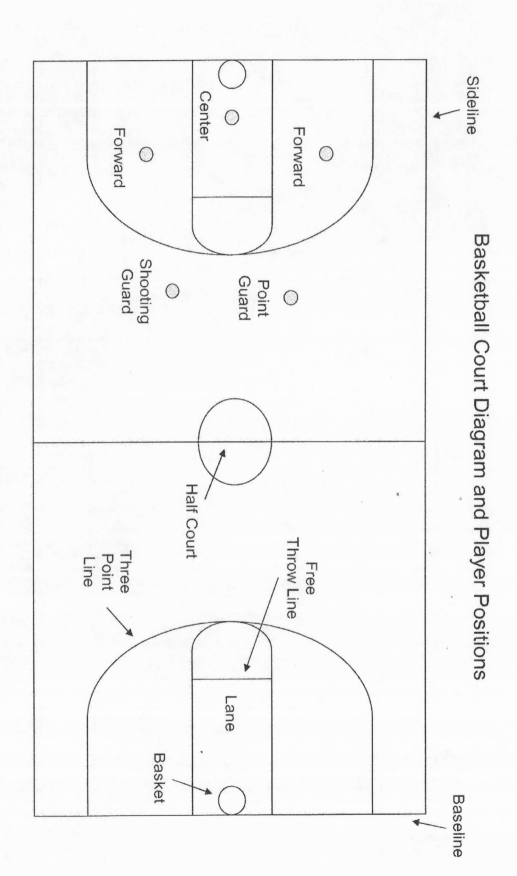

Basketball Court Diagram and Player Positions

Sideline

Center

Forward

Forward

Shooting
Guard

Point
Guard

Half Court

Three
Point
Line

Free
Throw Line

Lane

Basket

Baseline

Defensive Positioning

Basketball Positions

A basketball team is made up of 5 players on the court at a time. The players have offensive assignments when their team has the ball and defensive assignment when the opposing team has the ball. A description of each position is as follows:

Point Guard: the point guard is the primary ball handler. He brings the ball up court and directs the other players on the team on what play to run. His primary responsibility is to get the ball to the open player. On defense, he guards the opposing point guard trying to impede his progress and keeping him from making good passes. Point guards are typically smaller and quicker than other players with good ball handling skills and good vision of the court.

Shooting Guard: the shooting guard assists the point guard when bringing the ball up court. He is also usually the best outside shooter and counted on to make three point shots. On defense, he covers the other guard and tries to disrupt the offense. Shooting guards are usually good ball handlers and effective outside shooters being able to catch and release a shot quickly.

Forwards: Forwards are typically larger than the guards and work closer to the basket. They need to have the ability to penetrate to make lay-ups or pull-up for the short jump shots. On defense, they play closer to the basket trying to block shots and rebound the ball on missed shots.

Center: usually the tallest player on the team, the center plays closest to the basket and depended upon to make close range shots. He also needs to be able to rebound his teammates missed shots and put them back up into the basket. On defense, he plays very near the basket and tries to block opponents shots and rebound missed shots.

Basketball Terminology

1. **Bonus:** when a team reaches a certain number of fouls per half, the opposing team is awarded a free throw on the next non-shooting foul. If the player makes the first free throw he is awarded another free throw.

2. **Box out:** a term which refers to one playing positioning himself between an opposing player and the basket in order give him a better chance at a rebound.

3. **Dribble:** the act of bouncing the ball off the floor when a player has possession of it.

4. **Free throw:** Uncontested shot made from the free throw line that are worth 1 point each. Awarded to a player when he has been fouled.

5. **Field goal:** a basket made from anywhere on the floor. The basket is worth 2 or 3 points depending on the distance it was shot from.

6. **Held ball:** Used to be referred to as a "jump ball". This occurs when 2 opposing players gain control of the ball at the same time. The possession arrow determines which team gets the ball.

7. **Lane:** the rectangular area between the free throw line and the basket. Sometimes referred to as the "paint".

8. **Lay up:** a high percentage shot where the player bounces the ball off the backboard and into the basket from a very close distance.

9. **Man-to Man Defense:** a defense in which each player is responsible for covering an offensive player.

10. **Possession Arrow:** an alternating arrow displayed at the scorer's table that determines which team receives the ball to start a quarter or half and which team is awarded possession on a "held ball".

11. **Rebound:** occurs when a player gains possession of a missed shot by either team, can be an offensive or defensive rebound.

12. **Scorer's table:** situated at half court on the sideline, the scorer's table maintains the possession arrow, keeps up with the score and is the check-in point for any player entering the game.

13. **Screen:** a set play where an offensive player positions himself in a stationary position between a defensive player and the offensive player he is guarding.

14. **Three point shot:** a long shot attempted from beyond the three point line and is worth 3 points.

15. **Turnover:** occurs when a team loses possession of the ball and it is given to the other team.

16. **Zone Defense:** a defense where each player has responsibility for covering a certain area of the court, regardless of which offensive player is in the area.

17. **Penalties:** common rules infractions and the penalty assessed are as follows:

   A. Charge: a foul on the offensive player with the ball when he runs into a defender that is in a stationary position. The result is a turnover or a free throw for the other team if they are in the bonus.

   B. Double dribble: occurs when the player dribbling the ball touches it with two hands at the same time or stops dribbling and begins again. The result is a turnover.

   C. Foul: when a player makes physical contact with another player. The result is a turnover or a free throw for the other team if they are in the bonus.

   D. Moving screen: occurs when an offensive player tries to block a defensive play but has not become stationary. The result is a turnover or a free throw for the other team if they are in the bonus.

   E. Technical foul: a call made when a player behaves in a violent or belligerent manner or purposely makes a dangerous foul. The result is two free throws for the opposing team and possession of the ball. The player may be ejected from the game.

   F. Three second violation: called when an offensive player stands in the lane for more than 3 seconds without the ball. Results in a turnover.

G. <u>Traveling</u>: occurs when the offensive player dribbling the ball takes more than two steps without dribbling. Results in a turnover.

<u>READERS PLEASE NOTE</u>: There are many variations in formations and terminology for each sport and each player position. There are many informative websites for each sport. Just type the title of each section into your favorite search engine and you can learn more about each of these sports.

Coaches Corner

"Play Hard, Play Smart & Have Fun"

The purpose of this section is to give mothers a coach's perspective on youth sports. As a devoted father and an avid sports fan, coaching to me was the perfect combination of being able to spend quality time with my family and enjoying the thrill and excitement of being involved in athletics. Children can learn so many positive life lessons by being involved in sports that will stay with them for the rest of their life and can be beneficial in all aspects of their life.

We have all heard the horror stories of youth sports "gone bad", parents fighting in the stands, coaches verbally assaulting children for their performance, umpires being threatened by irate coaches and many other incidents that have resulted in negative press coverage. I would like to share with you my perspective on how youth sports should be conducted to insure the positive aspects of athletic participation are conveyed to our children.

I am not a coach by trade, only a coach by desire. I have been a volunteer coach for almost 15 years and coached baseball, basketball, hockey, football and soccer. I have coached numerous championship and All-star teams at various levels up to and into the high school level. My philosophy in coaching all the different sports is the same and very simple. I tell my kids that our goal is to "Play hard, play smart and have fun". When teams adopt this philosophy, winning is not gauged on the outcome of the games score but on the team's effort towards the accomplishment of their goal. It has been my experience that teams that approach the game in this manner inevitably are very successful in the win-loss column also.

There are very distinct levels of competitive play in youth sports, typically based on age. It is important that a parent understand the differences and expectations at the different levels. The following summary is only a guideline and can vary considerably from area to area.

5-8 Year Olds Recreation League Play

The teams in this age group typically play in non-competitive games. Official game scores are not kept although there will be a group of parents who will always keep score even if it not in the traditional manner (Ignore them). The focus of the coaches should be two-fold:

1) Teach the basic fundamentals of the game. Children can learn the proper way to play the game at this age. They may not have the physical skills

to always make the plays but they do have the mental ability to learn the fundamentals of the game and know what they should do.

2) Participation is critical. Playing time for all players should be kept as equal as possible regardless of skill level. It is the coaches and "PARENTS" responsibility to work with and improve the skill levels of their players. You can "make or break" a child's love for the game at this level. The most important lesson to learn at this stage is teamwork and for the children to understand that what is best for the team is not always the best for them personally.

<u>9-14 Year Old Recreation League Play</u>

This will be your child's first introduction into "officially" competitive games. Scores will be kept, team standings posted, league champions crowned and all-star teams selected. If you thought some parents went overboard in the lower age groups, "you ain't seen nothing yet". Rules for participation change and guidelines are typically in place to make sure each player receives some minimum amount of playing time. This is the age group when your child may only play the last two innings in right field and get up to bat once (Prepare yourself). If your child wants to play, it is very important that they work at the game outside of practice.

9-14 Year Old "Select or Traveling League" Play

Team competition in this league is taken to a whole other level. Players typically have to try-out, compete for spot on the team and may be cut. As a parent, you must be prepared for the commitment that will be expected from the coaches. These teams typically practice numerous times during the week and travel from county to county or state to state to compete on the weekends. There are no participation requirements and typically the only team goal is to "win". These teams are beneficial if your child has the desire, skills and dedication to the game. They will see a higher level of competition and it does provide some exposure that could be beneficial later if they have a desire to play at the "next level".

<u>15-18 Year Old High School Play</u>

Welcome to "big time" athletics. It has been my experience that this is when a lot of players begin to drop out of sports. The level of competition and the commitment that is expected from the athletes will generally weed out those players who don't truly have a love for their sport. This is the first time that your child will play for a coach who is being paid; up to this point all the coached have been volunteers. Your role as a parent will change dramatically. High school coaches will deal directly with the athletes and provide very little feedback and communication with the parents. Your primary responsibilities will include fundraising through the booster club and supporting your child away from the field. This can be a very rewarding experience for both parent and child and very well may be the last time your child plays organized sports. If you think of the progression through the age groups as a pyramid with professional sports being the top, your child has reached the top third of the pyramid at this point and very few go on to the next level of college athletics, let alone the pro's.

<u>"Assessing Your Coach"</u>

Coaches, like kids, come in all shapes, sizes and personalities. The following comparisons are based on my experiences and identify what you should look for in a coach as well as some warning signs which may alert you to the fact that you may need to find another team. Always remember that these coaches are volunteers!

Good Coaches Will:

1. Be organized with practice and game schedules.

2. Have a team mom to handle all non-coaching related activities such as team pictures, drinks assignments for practices and games and organizing team parties.

3. Be positive motivators encouraging participation from all players regardless of ability.

4. Teach the fundamentals of the game.

5. Conduct practices that use small group activities to keep players active and keep their attention.

6. Maintain control and discipline of their players by encouraging responsible behavior.

7. Encourage players to excel in the classroom as well as on the field

8. Teach players how to set goals and work to achieve them.

9. Stress that all players are important and can contribute to the team.

10. Encourage players to practice on their own to improve their skill level.

11. Teach the players the importance of eating and drinking properly.

12. Encourage players to rest properly the night before games.

13. Ensure the practices are conducted with the players safety in mind.

14. Make sports a positive, fun experience for the players.

Undesirable Coaches will:

1. Be late to practices or miss them altogether.
2. Not communicate game or practice schedule changes.
3. Scream, holler and otherwise make a fool of themselves to players, referees, other coaches and parents.
4. Use intimidation or other tactics to keep the players in line.
5. Focus on the good players and give little help or playing time to less skilled players.
6. Coach to win at all costs without regard to playing time of the players.
7. Teach players dirty tricks or unsportsmanlike play to gain an advantage.
8. Disregard unsafe play or conditions.
9. Focus on their own child and make him the star of the team even if he is not a very skilled player.
10. Conduct very ineffective practices because they haven't prepared properly.
11. Take the love of the game away from players.

What You Need To Know If
Your Child Plays On!!

Sports Moms Advice on Securing Scholarship Money

Most everyone is aware of the escalating cost of college tuition. Do not count on athletic scholarship money to cover your child's expenses. If they are fortunate enough to receive an athletic scholarship, they are normally limited in what they will cover leaving many expenses for you to cover. There are athletes that do get a "full ride" but they are the exception and not the rule. The good news is that there is significant scholarship money available for students with good academic performance. This also applies if your child decides not to play sports at the collegiate level. The guidelines below come from my experience in evaluating colleges and universities for my son's education:

- SAT scores and GPA translate directly into scholarship money. The higher the GPA and the SAT, the more money they will qualify for.
- Although both are important, schools prefer a student with a high GPA and lower SAT score over a student with a high SAT score and a lower GPA. The GPA signifies what type of work ethic the student has.
- Insure your child understands that good grades in high school translate into money. I have impressed upon my younger son that he can make $20,000 a year or more in scholarship money by making good grades.
- Have your child take the SAT early and often. The final score used is taken from the best scores on the different sections and combined.
- Begin seriously looking in the summer of their Junior year and schedule campus visits to the schools of your choice.
- Consider all colleges both public and private. Don't let the sticker price of private institutions scare you away. Many offer substantial scholarships.
- Narrow down you choices and contact the Financial Aid offices of those selected.
- Our best success was working directly with the Financial Aid to determine the amount of aid available.

- Starting the process early helps you determine deadlines for certain scholarships. You should start contacting the offices in the early fall of their Senior year.

- The Admissions office will schedule campus visits. This is a good time to schedule a meeting with the coach and they can usually arrange this.

- Coaches like student athletes that qualify for academic scholarship money. They are more likely to do well in class and maintain eligibility and they can save the athletic money for gifted athletes that have not had as good academic performance.

- Division III schools may be a great opportunity for your child even though they don't give athletic scholarships. That's why academics are so important.

- Finally, remember when comparing schools, the quality of education is the most important. Their playing days will come to an end but the education will last them a lifetime.

Ten Steps to Becoming a College Athlete

1. Register with the NCAA (National Collegiate Athletic Association). This should be done if they are considering a division I or II School. Ask your high school coach about getting the Guide for the College Bound Student Athlete from the NCAA.

2. Keep up with all accomplishments during High School. These should be athletic and academic. There is a worksheet in the back of the book.

3. Make a "brag sheet". You will find a good example of one in the back of the book.

4. Start visiting the colleges or Universities you are interested in. Go to their games and or attend their sports camps.

5. Starting in the 9th grade stress GPA! This is probably the most important of the ten. Their grade point average is money in or out of your pocket in the way of academic scholarships.

6. Consider traveling or club teams. The high school teams do not get the exposure that the traveling teams do. Many major tournaments are held just for exposure.

7. Write letters and or make videos to send to coaches. You also need to ask teachers and coaches to write letters of recommendation to mail to the college with your packet of information, don't forget to include your transcripts.

8. Consider all schools regardless of division or cost. Schools are very helpful with financial aid no matter what the size.

9. Attend any offered college information seminars. This is a good way to learn what schools require and about financial aid programs available.

10. Encourage non athletic extra curricular activities. These could be the deciding factor in acceptance of the college of your choice.

Remember playing at the college level is like icing on the cake. Don't get caught up in the wrong way of thinking. Take a hard look at what matters to you and your college bound child in the long run—<u>a college</u> <u>education</u>. The odds of them becoming a professional athlete are unlikely.

DUSTY LUEBBERS

123 Sportsmans Way
LaGrange, GA 30240
Home: (706) 555-1234
email@yahoo.com
LaGrange Academy Warriors
Head Coach: Charles Parker
Home: (706) 555-1235 School: (706) 555-1236

2003 OFFENSIVE STATS

AB	Ave	Slg%	OB%	1	2	3	HR	RBI	BB	HBP	SO
60	0.485	0.982	0.654	12	10	0	7	28	12	6	4

➢ Position(s): P, SS, 2nd, 3rd, CF   Bats R, Throws R
➢ Very Versatile: Played 5 positions in one game
➢ Great Contact Hitter: Swung and missed 3 times all season

"You've made plays I only see on ESPN"

Coach Antwan Smith – Florida State Baseball Camp

Baseball Awards

2003   All County – LaGrange Daily News
     All State (honorable mention) – GISA Class AA
     All Region – GISA Region 4AA
     Hustle Award – LaGrange Academy
     Coaches Award – LaGrange Academy
2002   All Region – GISA Region 4AA
     Most Valuable Player – LaGrange Academy
2001   Gold Glove Award – LaGrange Academy
2000   Gold Glove Award – LaGrange Academy

Basketball Awards

2002-03   All Region (honorable mention) – GISA Region 4AA
     Best Defensive Player – Lagrange Academy
2001-02   Hustle Award – LaGrange Academy

Extracurricular Activities

Interact Club –10th, 11th, 12th

Young Life – 10th, 11th, 12th

Coca Cola Fundraiser Drive – 10th

Fellowship of Christian Athletes

National Youth Coaches Association Assistant Coach

Leadership Nominations

Hugh O'Brien Award – 10th   Troup Leadership – 11th

National Young Leaders Conference – 12th

MOST OUTSTANDING MALE SENIOR

Lagrange Optimist Club

Academic Achievements

GPA – 3.4, 1150 on SAT

Graduation Date: May 2004

Academic Honors – 9th, 10th, 11th

Beta Honors Club – 9th, 10th, 11th

Dual Enrollment – LaGrange College

"Who's Who Among America's High School Students"

LaGrange Academy's Dusty Luebbers is congratulated after hitting a leadoff home run against Tiftarea in the second game of their series Monday. The Warriors won 11-0 to even the series at one game apiece.

Club or Activity	9th	10th	11th	12th

Use this sheet to keep up with the High School years.
List in this section clubs, sports and community service your child has participated in.
Place a check mark in the column of the grade they were in at the time they were involved in the activity.

About the Author

Tracey and her husband Marty met in high school when they were 16 years old. She was the Captain of the cheerleading squad and he was a corner back for the football team. Through out their childhood each of them had participated in many sports. They were married in 1983 one year after high school graduation. Two years later Dusty was born. Marty went on to Florida State University and graduated with an engineering degree. Soon after he graduated they moved to LaGrange Georgia. Dusty showed an interest in baseball among other sports at a very young age. Eric was born 3 ½ years later and had the same interest in sports as big brother had. Each of the boys grew up to play many sports. Marty was the usually the coach and Tracey the team mom. As the two boys grew older each chose the one sport they loved the most. For Dusty it was baseball and for Eric it was soccer. Sometimes with two games going on at the same time and in different locations Tracey learned how to manage it all and still keep it fun.

They live in LaGrange Georgia with their two sons. Dusty attends LaGrange College majoring in biology and plans to become an orthopedic surgeon, he also plays baseball for the college. Eric attends Troup County High School and plays soccer for the school, he is also a member of the Troup Titans Select Soccer Club.

The Luebbers are still loving it and going strong!

Made in the USA
Lexington, KY
12 December 2009